FLOWERS
FOR ALL SEASONS
SUMMER

FLOWERS
FOR ALL SEASONS
SUMMER

Text by Jane Packer and Elizabeth Wilhide

Fawcett Columbine · New York

A Fawcett Columbine Book
Published by Ballantine Books

Copyright © 1989 by Pavilion Books

All rights reserved under International and Pan-American
copyright conventions. Published in the United States
by Ballantine Books, a division of Random House, Inc.,
New York.

Published in Great Britain by Pavilion Books

Packer, Jane. 1959–
Flowers for all seasons: summer/
Jane Packer.—1st American ed.

p. cm.
ISBN 0-449-90412-1
1. Flower arrangement. 2. Flowers. 3. Summer. I. Title.
SB449.P224 1989
745.92—dc19   88-26833
                                 CIP

Manufactured in Spain
by Cayfosa Industria Grafica
First American Edition: May 1989

10 9 8 7 6 5 4 3 2 1

Contents

Introduction

Summer is the flower arranger's delight. It is the one season of the year which really works with you: colours are rich and varied, foliage lush and abundant, and gardens come into their own. There is simply more of everything.

The summer months are a time for holidays and outdoor events, such as fêtes, barbecues and garden parties. Above all, it is the season of weddings. As I particularly enjoy wedding work, summer is a special time of year for me.

With all this abundance and variety, there is no pressing reason why anyone should need to extend the summer palette with imports or commercially cultivated flowers. It can be especially satisfying, as well as appropriate, to try to express the mood of the season in the style of your displays. In fact, nothing could be easier. Vibrant, rich shades emphasize the warmth of a sunny day; a mass of colour has all the cheerfulness of a summer meadow; an all-white arrangement looks refreshing and cool in the long summer evenings. Whatever colour scheme you require it can be found in the wide range of summer flowers.

As far as the style of displays is concerned, summer flowers promote a natural, lush look. Since there are more flowers and foliage, it is easy and cheap to create massed displays. Nothing has to be precise – the whole effect can be overgrown and trailing, suggesting a mood of happy relaxation rather than formal elegance. Towards the end of the summer, seasonal fruits and vegetables can lend their own vitality and interest to arrangements: a traditional cottage garden harmony.

Summer is a time when we like to feel closer to the outdoors, eating outside as often as the weather allows, opening windows wide and generally spending more time in the garden. Even if your flowers have come from a florist's rather than your own flower bed, they are an important means of reinforcing this link with nature.

JANE PACKER

Left: A full summery arrangement of delphiniums, scabious, larkspur, copper beech, ferns and blackberries tones with blue and white china.

Summer Flowers and Foliage

Summer offers great scope for creativity. There are not only more species available, but there is also tremendous variety within each – many more colours, sizes and shapes of flowers. Warm weather means outdoor growing, which in turn means that prices come down in flower shops. Many arrangements can be created for next to nothing if you can use the garden as a source of supplementary foliage.

Summer flowers tend to be soft and flowing. Even tall upright species such as delphinium, larkspur and nigella have wispy sideshoots which break the line. Flowering vines such as jasmine, clematis and honeysuckle are naturally trailing and climbing, while spray flowers have an inbuilt bushiness. All of this lushness can be given extra emphasis by foliage cut from garden shrubs. Derelict sites can be a good source of weeds, such as old man's beard, or buddleia (butterfly bush), both of which are useful fillers. Many summer flowers are scented, often with a sweet, lingering perfume rather than the fruity smell of spring flowers.

One disadvantage of summer is that flowers generally have a short life, especially those from the garden which have not been commercially treated. But availability and low cost mean that this is not too much of a drawback. Take care over positioning and conditioning to help prolong the life of your arrangements.

SELECTING FLOWERS

Buying in bud is advisable for most flowers: it is better to select flowers which are still in bud to make the most of their short life. Avoid tight green buds which may never open and opt for those just beginning to show colour.

Always check any flowers wrapped in cellophane for signs of botrytis or mildew. Flowers which have been

Right: Striking pewter and glass Art Nouveau vases are enhanced by a tall display of stock and blue aconitum (monkshood), supplemented by ivy trails and green beech leaves. Individual stock florets have been placed among the strands of ivy.

kept wrapped for several days will sweat because of the lack of ventilation and stems and foliage will begin to rot. In summer, this process will be accelerated because of the heat.

To get the best from your flowers, buy them early in the day and take them straight home for conditioning. If you are cutting flowers from your garden, you should also cut early in the day when it is cooler.

SOURCES

A good florist is the best source for healthy fresh flowers and will stock a wider range of colours and varieties than the average market stall or corner shop. Shops which only carry flowers as a sideline – petrol stations, for example – may be less reliable. A lack of trained staff and a slower turnover of stock can lead to flowers being displayed when they are past their best.

Florists' flowers used to be synonymous with highly cultivated hothouse blooms, to the extent that when "garden" flowers became more commonly available in

Above left: Yellow and pink are often considered to be clashing colours, but nature can combine them to great effect, as in the particular variety of yellow and pink honeysuckle used in this arrangement. Miniature pink roses and achillea pick out the same two shades, also echoed in the plates and bowls.

shops, people showed a certain reluctance to buy them. With fashion now swinging away from the formal and exotic in favour of natural effects, there is less of a distinction between what you can see growing in a garden and what is on sale in a flower shop. The biggest difference is that many flowers appear much earlier in the flower shops than they do in the garden, by virtue of the flowers being commercially cultivated or flown in from warmer areas. And, of course, florists can supply many types of flower virtually all year round, which act as a useful supplement to the seasonal range.

Planning and planting a garden to create a source of cut flowers for the home is a subject in itself. But unless beds and borders are overflowing with blooms, most people have to compromise between having colour indoors or out. During the summer, this may be less of a problem; cutting annuals and perennials stimulates flower production. Cutting flowering shrubs or trees amounts to pruning; there is the temptation to remove the most luxuriant branch for your display at the expense of the plant. Most gardens, however, can well stand a little cropping and the flowers and foliage you have grown yourself are especially satisyfing.

Not only gardens, but also hedgerows, verges and neglected patches of land can provide plentiful sources of humble but attractive flowers and foliage, such as buddleia, old man's beard and ivy. Common meadow flowers such as poppies and daisies always look charming and fresh. Aside from these common or invasive species, however, wild flowers should never be picked. Areas of true woodland, wild meadows and hedgerows are fast declining, with the loss of many species and it is important to leave the flowers and plants untouched to aid their conservation.

The Summer Palette

ACHILLEA
Availability May–September; cut
Price Cheap
Colour range White, pink, peach, red, mustard, yellow
Life span Long-lasting
The mustard-coloured variety is the most common. Easy to grow and easy to dry; the flat heads are useful as space fillers.

AGAPANTHUS (African lily; *Agapanthus africanus*)
Availability June–September; cut
Price Medium
Colour range Blue and white
Life span Long-lasting
Usually available long-stemmed; very large but delicate-looking globular heads, good for displaying in tall vases or large arrangements. Vivid green, thick tubular stems are excellent in see-through containers.

ALCHEMILLA (Lady's mantle; *Alchemilla mollis*)
Availability May–August; cut or from garden
Price Cheap
Colour range Bright green-yellow
Life span Long-lasting
Easily grown in the garden, alchemilla is an excellent filler for arrangements. The vivid colour mixes well with other colours.

ALLIUM (flowery onion; *Allium* spp.)
Availability May–September; cut
Price Cheap
Colour range Purple or white
Life span Very long-lasting
Foliage-free bright green stems suit clear containers. Change water daily as it will discolour quickly and smell pungently of onion.

ALSTROEMERIA (Peruvian lily; *Alstroemeria* hybrids)
Availability Year-round (cut); summer only for bright yellow garden variety
Price Cheap to medium
Colour range Purple, red, peach, pink, yellow, white
Life span Long-lasting
Main flowers die off, but buds continue to open. Resembles an orchid, so flowers look more expensive than they are. Good for full displays or low arrangements and bridal bouquets.

ANTIRRHINUM (Snapdragon; *Antirrhinum majus*)
Availability May–August (cut); commercially, year-round
Price Medium
Colour range Red, purple, orange, pink, yellow, white
Life span Long-lasting
A lovely flower for country or cottage-type displays mixed with other summer flowers. It is available long-stemmed, but it is also excellent cut short for full basket arrangements.

ASTILBE (Spirea; *Astilbe* hybrids)
Availability May–September; cut
Price Medium
Colour range White, pink, dark pink, red
Life span Short
The feathery plume is lovely in either vase displays or arrangements; best mixed with other varieties to create a country feel.

BEECH (*Fagus* spp.)
Availability May–September; cut
Price Cheap
Colour range Green or copper
Life span Long-lasting
The early spring shoots of green beech are vivid; copper beech leaves mix well with rich pinks to create a vibrant warm display. Tends to dry out quickly in oasis.

BOUVARDIA (*Bouvardia* spp.)
Availability Year-round; cut
Price Expensive
Colour range Red, pink, dark pink, yellow, white
Life span Short
Dainty grouping of florets at tip of long stem. Needs to be treated with care; can wilt in a draught or if deprived of water for a period. Best used in a vase rather than oasis. Avoid using in wedding bouquets.

BUDDLEIA (Butterfly bush; *Buddleia davidii*)
Availability July – October; easily obtained from garden
Price Free from garden
Colour range Purple or white
Life span Long-lasting
The fragrant plumes attract butterflies in the garden. Gives a country look to vase displays or large arrangements.

CAMPANULA (Bellflower; *Campanula* spp.)
Availability May–August; cut
Price Cheap
Colour range Blues, mauve, white
Life span Long-lasting
Beautiful ice blue or white flowers, covering two-thirds of the stem; good for vase and oasis displays.

13

CELOSIA (*Celosia argentea*)
Availability June–August; cut
Price Expensive
Colour range Yellow, pink, purple, red
Life span Long-lasting
Large, unusual flower head with the appearance of crushed velvet – unconventional beauty makes this one for the flower connoisseur. Cut short to use as a filler or use long in dramatic displays. Remove foliage as it wilts early; dries well.

CHRYSANTHEMUM (*Chrysanthemum morifolium* varieties)
Availability Year-round; cut or potted
Price Cheap to medium
Colour range White, cream, pink, peach, bronze, yellow, red, purple
Life span Very long-lasting
Enormous range of colour and varieties; double, single, spider, sprays and large blooms. Excellent for arrangements that need to last a long time.

CLEMATIS (*Clematis* spp.)
Availability May–September; cut from garden
Price Free
Colour range White, pink, purple
Life span Short
Trails of clematis are wonderful to use in all sizes of arrangements, both in a vase or oasis. Softens the formal lines of any display. Although flower life is short, the vines are useful for trailing effects, especially mauve-tinged foliage of *montana rubens*. Lasts well in water.

CORNFLOWER (*Centaurea cyanus*)
Availability May–August; cut
Price Cheap
Colour range White, pink, light blue, dark blue
Life span Short
These vivid blues are popular for wedding bouquets. Looks good either alone or mixed with other flowers.

DELPHINIUM (*Delphinium elatum* hybrids)
Availability May–September; cut
Price Expensive (tall stems)
Colour range White, cream, blue, pink (red in experimental stage)
Life span Long-lasting
Long-stemmed spires look stunning in tall vases, either alone or mixed to create abundant summer displays.

ECHINOPS (Globe-thistle; *Echinops ritro*)
Availability June–September; cut
Price Cheap
Colour range Blue or white
Life span Very long-lasting
An interesting, rather than a pretty flower; easily dried. Because it is cheap, it is good for filling large arrangements.

ELAEAGNUS (*Elaeagnus* spp.)
Availability Year-round; cut
Price Medium
Colour range Yellow and green foliage
Life span Long-lasting
Foliage shrubs, such as this one, are invaluable in the flower arranger's garden. The interesting colours and leaf shape are excellent for arrangements and will last well in wedding bouquets.

EREMURUS (Foxtail-lily; *Eremurus* spp.)
Availability June–August, cut
Price Expensive
Colour range White, yellow, orange
Life span Very long-lasting
Very long stems. Florets continue to open right to tip of flower head. Makes a strong statement in tall vase displays; also good for large pedestal arrangements. Not good cut short.

ERYNGIUM (*Eryngium* spp.)
Availability May–September: cut
Price Medium
Colour range Blue, silver
Life span Long-lasting
Interesting spiky, teasel-like heads. Best used as part of a mixture for a country look; not particularly effective on its own. Can be dried easily.

FOXGLOVE (*Digitalis purpurea*)
Availability May-June; cut from florist or garden
Price Expensive or free (if cut from garden)
Colour range Pink to purple
Life span Medium
Beautiful tall-stemmed flower. Now available commercially, so avoid picking in the wild. Can be seeded and grown in the garden.

GERANIUM (*Pelargonium* spp.)
Availability May–September; cut from garden or potted
Price Cheap
Colour range White, pink, peach, purple, red
Life span Long-lasting
Snipping flower heads from plants will not stop new blooms appearing throughout the summer. Lemon geranium has a marvellous scent.

GERBERA (Transvaal-daisy; *Gerbera jamesonii*)
Availability Year-round; cut
Price Medium
Colour range White, pink, yellow, peach, red, purple
Life span Long-lasting
Large, exotic daisy-like flower. If stems are soft, they will stiffen in water but in a bent shape. To straighten, support upright in a tub of deep water before placing flowers in a vase or arrangement.

GLADIOLUS (Sword lily; *Gladiolus* hybrids)
Availability June–December; cut
Price Cheap
Colour range White, cream, pink, yellow, orange, red, green
Life span Long-lasting
Elegant long-stemmed flower. Remove old flowers as new buds open at tip of the stem. Look modern in tall glass vases or use in mixed arrangements. Individual florets are excellent for bridal work.

GODETIA (*Clarkia* spp.)
Availability June; cut
Price Cheap
Colour range Red, pink, mauve, peach in mixed bunches
Life span Long-lasting
Normally a short-stemmed flower; lasts very well if you remove wilting flowers and allow buds space to open. Change water regularly. Remove all side stems below water level as they will deteriorate quickly.

GOLDEN ROD (*Solidago* hybrids)
Availability May–July; cut
Price Cheap or cut from garden
Colour range Yellow
Life span Long-lasting
Grows well in garden; also abundant in the wild. Buy or pick when florets are green – they open to mustard yellow. Remove foliage from the stem as it decays in water quickly. Easy to dry.

GYPSOPHILA (Baby's breath; *Gypsophila*)
Availability Year-round; cut
Price Cheap
Colour range White; pink in summer only
Life span Long-lasting
Always buy with open florets; tight buds rarely open. Extremely popular for wedding bouquets (to the point of being a cliché) as it gives a light lacy effect to any arrangement.

HONEYSUCKLE (*Lonicera* spp.)
Availability May–August; cut
Price Usually cut from garden
Colour range Cream, pink, yellow, peach
Life span Long-lasting
Honeysuckle has a delicious perfume. Its trailing strands make it invaluable for informal displays, wedding bouquets or to soften the lines of a more formal arrangement.

HOSTA (*Hosta* spp.)
Availability May–August; cut
Price Usually cut from garden
Colour range Many greens, variegated green-white or green-yellow
Life span Long-lasting
A must for the flower-arranger's garden (but it must be protected from slugs who love the broad fleshy leaves). Just a few leaves can create a good base to an arrangement.

HYDRANGEA (*Hydrangea* spp.)
Availability May–Sept; cut
Price Medium
Colour range White, pink, blue, purple and green
Life span Long-lasting
Not readily available from florists as cut flowers; garden is a good source of supply. Individual bracts are good for wedding work; full heads make a good filler for any display. Easily dried.

IVY (*Hedera* spp.)
Availability Year-round
Price Cheap
Colour range Dark green; variegated white and yellow
Life span Long-lasting
Freely grows in the wild and most florists or garden centres stock plants. Useful trailing foliage in any display or wedding arrangement. Wide mix of varieties.

JASMINE (*Jasminum* spp.)
Availability June–October, or year-round from florist
Price Expensive
Colour range White, pink, yellow
Life span Long-lasting
Beautifully scented flower. When flowers have disappeared, delicate foliage trails are useful for extending line of arrangements and in wedding work. Another plus for the flower arranger's garden.

LARKSPUR (*Consolida* sp.)
Availability May–August; cut
Price Cheap
Colour range White, pink, blue
Life span Short
A traditional garden flower, with soft, delicate-looking blooms. Soft pastel colour range to deep blue; perfect for cottage-type displays. Easy to dry.

LAVATERA
Availability June–August; cut
Price Cheap
Colour range White, pink, purple
Life span Short
Very delicate, translucent, bell-shaped flowers. Buds will continue to open. Best used in country-style arrangements.

LAVENDER (*Lavandula* sp.)
Availability June–August; cut
Price Expensive (but available from garden)
Colour range Pale lavender to dark purple
Life span Long-lasting
Good flower to dry for use in pot-pourri or pomanders. Dry by hanging upside down; use the flakes of flowers in pot-pourri or tie stems wheatsheaf-style. Characteristically scented.

MARGUERITE (*Chrysanthemum frutescens*)
Availability May–September; cut
Price Cheap
Colour range White and yellow
Life span Long-lasting
These clean, bright daisies instantly evoke summer. Use on their own for a modern look; mix for country displays. Bushes or standard plants look wonderful on the patio.

MARIGOLD (*Tagetes* spp.)
Availability April–August; cut or potted
Price Cheap
Colour range Yellow, orange, burnt orange
Life span Long-lasting
Vivid, fun-looking flower with an interesting aroma. Can be used in salads and as culinary decoration. Strong, vegetable scent.

MOLUCELLA (Bells of Ireland; *Molucella laevis*)
Availability June–August; cut
Price Cheap
Colour range Green, with white florets inside bells
Life span Long-lasting
A vivid green foliage-type flower with a sharp smell. Arcs gently; can be used in modern or garden-type displays. Dries well.

MONTBRETIA (*Crocosmia* sp.)
Availability May–July; cut
Price Cheap
Colour range Orange
Life span Long-lasting
Bright orange flowers similar to freesias; foliage similar to miniature gladioli. Montbretia has a strong appearance used on its own in a vase; also mixes well with other colours in summer combinations.

NICOTIANA (Flowering tobacco; *Nicotiana* spp.)
Availability April–August; cut or potted
Price Cheap
Colour range White, pink, red, purple, green
Life span Long-lasting
Traditional cottage-garden plant which contrives to flower throughout the summer, well-loved for its heady evening perfume. The flowers of modern varieties stay open all day, making them much more useful to flower arrangers, but have lost most of their scent. Whole plant is sticky to the touch.

NIGELLA (Love-in-a-mist; *Nigella damascena*)
Availability May–July; cut
Price Cheap
Colour range Blue, pink or white
Life span Short life
The common name, with its romantic connotations, perfectly describes the beautiful delicate petals surrounded by a haze of tendrils. Easy to dry; when flowers drop, seed heads remain, which are also useful in arrangements and can be dried.

PANSY (*Viola* sp.)
Availability April–September; potted
Price Cheap
Colour range Almost every colour and colour combination
Life span Long-lasting
Old-fashioned flower, normally available as bedding plant for window boxes from late spring.
Also delightful indoors in baskets or pottery bowls.

PEONY (*Paeonia* hybrids)
Availability May–June; cut
Price Cheap
Colour range White, cream, pink, red
Life span Short
Short season, depending on the elements. A wonderfully luscious flower with a slight perfume best used open rather than in bud; always buy buds which are beginning to show colour, not tight green ones. Traditional garden flower; can look oriental if restricted to an arrangement of a few blooms.

PHLOX (*Phlox paniculata* hybrids)
Availability May–August; cut
Price Cheap
Colour range White, pink, cerise, purple
Life span Short
Cottage garden flower; good for country-style arrangements. Strong, distinctive perfume, although commercial flowers have no scent.

POPPY (*Papaver* spp.)
Availability May–August; cut. December–February; commercially grown
Price Cheap
Colour range White, pink, peach, red; grey poppy heads
Life span Short
A delicate flower, most readily available as a cut flower in strong shades, or from the garden. Old-fashioned appearance; bare seed heads are also interesting in arrangements.

PINK (*Dianthus* sp.)
Availability May–August; cut
Price Cheap
Colour range White, pink, lilac, cerise, nearly red
Life span Long-lasting
Sweet perfumed flower with old-fashioned sentimental associations. Readily available from florist and easy to grow in garden. Buy flowers which are open but without centre stamens visible. Excellent for wedding work.

RUDBECKIA (Coneflower; *Rudbeckia* spp.)
Availability June–August; cut
Price Cheap
Colour range Yellow to orange
Life span Short life
Cottage-garden flower. When petals begin to look jaded, you can remove and use brown thistle-like centre as an interesting component in arrangements.

SCABIOUS (Pincushion flower; *Scabiosa caucasica*)
Availability May–August; cut
Price Cheap
Colour range Blue, white
Life span Short
Scabious, one of my favourite flowers, immediately suggests a country garden. Blue is the most common variety. Buy when the centre florets are in green bud.

SEDUM (Stonecrop; *Sedum* spp.)
Availability July–August
Price Cheap
Colour range Green to pink
Lifespan Long-lasting
Easily grown, fleshy plant with the added advantage of attracting butterflies. A good filler for arrangements, but not for use alone. Lasts well, but stems will begin to deteriorate quickly so change water regularly.

PRIVET (*Ligustrum* spp.)
Availability Year-round
Price Cheap
Colour range Lime green, variegated, dark green
Life span Long-lasting
Popular hedging plant and therefore often overlooked. A reliable foliage for arrangements.

ROSE (*Rosa* hybrids)
Availability Year-round; cut
Price Cheap to expensive
Colour range Wide variety of colours
Life span Long-lasting
Commercially grown roses normally lack scent. Early wilting or head dropping can be avoided by trimming stems, placing 2 inches (5cm) of stem in boiling water for 20 seconds to clear air blocks and then placing roses in deep water for several hours. Cut short for cottage look, long-stemmed for sophistication.

SENECIO (Dusky miller; *Senecio* spp.)
Availability May–September; cut
Price Medium
Colour range Silver foliage
Life span Long-lasting
Not easy to find in florists' but easy to grow in garden. A bonus for flower arrangers.

SKIMMIA (*Skimmia japonica*)
Availability Year-round; cut
Price Medium
Colour range Gold to green, red
Life span Long-lasting
In late summer this shrub produces bud-like flowers. Creates a sense of texture in arrangement; gardens are best source.

SPIRAEA (*Spiraea* spp.)
Availability May–August; cut
Price Medium
Colour range White, pink, yellow
Life span Long-lasting
There is a range of flower colours – the season begins with white. Airy flower sprays drop flake-like petals, so avoid using in arrangements near food.

STOCK (*Matthiola incana*)
Availability May–July; cut
Price Cheap to expensive
Colour range White, cream, pink, cerise, lilac, purple
Life span Long-lasting
Stock has a wonderful scent and makes a good filler. Crumpled petals are a characteristic; translucent flowers are a sign of age. Stock sweats badly so avoid bunched packages in cellophane. Change water frequently to prevent it smelling.

SUNFLOWER (*Helianthus* spp.)
Availability July–August; cut
Price Cheap
Colour range Yellow
Life span Long-lasting
Bold flower, especially good for large arrangements or for a focal point. Not readily available as a cut flower but easy to grow in garden.

SWEET PEA (*Lathyrus odoratus*)
Availability May–July; cut
Price Expensive (commercial)
Colour range White, pink, peach, cream, cerise, lilac, purple, red
Life span Short
Commercial varieties are available with long stems and in shades such as peach, unknown in the garden. Also treated to extend life. Wonderful perfume; delicate, oriental appearance.

SWEET WILLIAM (*Dianthus barbatus*)
Availability May–July; cut
Price Cheap
Colour range White, pink, red, purple
Life span Long-lasting
Traditional cottage-garden flower. Buds will continue to open if old flowers are removed from the heavy clusters.

TRACHELIUM (*Trachelium caeruleum*)
Availability April–August; cut
Price Medium
Colour range Blue, white
Life span Long-lasting
Hazy-looking cluster of florets at the end of thin stems. The blue variety is preferable to the white, which can look greyish.

YEAR-ROUND FLOWERS
Although some of the following flowers and foliage are associated with a particular season, they are generally available year-round from florists and flower stalls, and make a useful supplement to the typical seasonal range.
*indicates description in text.

ALSTROEMERIA	CYPRESSUS	*GYPSOPHILA	LILY
BOX	EUCALYPTUS	IRIS	MOSS
CARNATION	FREESIA	*IVY	ORCHID
*CHRYSANTHEMUM	*GLADIOLUS	LAUREL	*ROSE

A Style for Summer

Flowers are always a welcome sight, but in summer they truly come into their own. In winter, a mass of hothouse blooms can appear contrived and indulgent, but a similar quantity of summer flowers is merely fresh and spontaneous. With all the abundance and variety in the garden, even a group of several large well-filled vases does not look extravagant.

The breadth of choice allows you to adopt almost any approach when it comes to display. Since summer flowers are so simple to arrange, it is not difficult to create "natural" effects with a mixture of species. The range of colours means that you can easily coordinate flowers with decoration if you want. Impromptu gestures – scattering petals on tabletops, combining fruit with flower heads, adding green vegetables from the garden to displays, all of which might be slightly pretentious at other times of the year – suit the informal summer mood and add a sense of vitality and surprise.

Above left: A traditional triangular-shaped arrangement has been softened by the use of trails of jasmine and lush, summery flowers. Phlox, antirrhinum, azalea, lily buds, celosia and 'La Minuet' roses (a white variety with a pink tinge) have been assembled in shades of pink and red.

Right: Summer is the time for spontaneous gestures. A plain earthenware pot in a doorway, filled with delphiniums and other garden flowers, suggests the freshness and abundance of the summer garden.

FLOWERS FOR THE HOME

The natural approach to flower arranging means more than just avoiding stiff, contrived displays; the type which always look as if an important event were about to take place. More fundamentally, it means treating flowers as a natural extension of your tastes and preferences — in fact, as part of your life. You may not be able to afford large quantities of fresh flowers every week, but when you do create a display it should look like it belongs, rather than appearing awkward and inappropriate. To achieve this quality of spontaneity, flowers should appear to be at ease in their surroundings, complementing colours and mood.

In the summer, no one need feel self-conscious about having flowers around the house; it is all part of the general outward-looking and relaxed mood. And you can get away with larger quantities, too — more flowers and more arrangements — than you can in cold, greyer months. In late winter or early spring, when little is happening in the garden and the trees are still bare, even a small display has great impact. In the summer, however, a few blooms can easily be overlooked. Massing flowers, positioning displays for maximum impact and adopting bold colour combinations will ensure flowers are noticed. But a *little* restraint is required — the effect should not be overpowering.

Left: Delicate pastel shades and a mixture of small, dainty flowers give this bouquet of cornflowers, scabious, aster and campanula an impulsive, almost wild look.

Right: A blaze of vivid colour shows up well in the bright summer light. Marigolds, achillea, honeysuckle, roses, phlox, azalea and jasmine have been arranged in oasis in a low, wide basket — the style of container echoing the wicker furniture.

COLOUR

Summer presents few difficulties when it comes to matching the colour of flowers to room decoration, coordinating with the colours of rugs, upholstery, curtain fabric or paintings, for example. But there are other possibilities. You can bring out the feeling of light and heat by choosing colours from the warm spectrum — reds, yellows and oranges. Vivid clashes of these hot colours are stunning, evocative of the unusual combinations seen in the textiles and ceramics of Latin America, India and the Mediterranean. Alternatively, "cooler" displays, using whites, silvers and pale blues, will show up well in the fading evening light.

Mixing flower colours is the key to summer-style informality. Even commercial roses lose some of their hothouse refinement when grouped in cheerful colour combinations of yellow, pink and red, rather than tastefully coordinated. Because the light is brighter in the summer, more positive shades can be used — subtlety may well be lost under a noonday glare.

POSITION

In the summer, life span is a particularly critical issue. Commercial flowers are often treated to prolong their life, but garden species are not and will die much more quickly. If your arrangement consists of a large proportion of garden flowers, it is especially important to be careful where it is positioned. Avoid window sills, where the heat is most intense, kitchen counters near heat sources such as hobs and ovens, and steamy bathrooms. Unused fireplaces are always good locations, both from a practical and aesthetic point of view, as are hallways, where flowers not only provide a welcoming sight but also benefit from the lower temperature. One other practical consideration: do not place large displays directly in a main route where they may be upset.

The aesthetic rules for positioning are just a matter of common sense. The key is eyeline. Mantelpieces suit displays that are meant to be viewed from standing height — as you enter a room, for example. Because so many summer flowers are trailing species, arrangements

Right: A golden, glowing table centre exaggerates the warmth of the yellow walls and polished mahogany. Large sunflowers are cut low and used in the centre of the display. Fennel fronds, rowanberries, goldenrod, molucella and rudbeckia are also included.

often need to be placed fairly high up where you can appreciate the full extent of the display. Tall upright flowers such as delphiniums or larkspur benefit from having their height emphasized — by displaying them against an elegant sash window or in a high-ceiling room, for example. Low-level arrangements, using short flowers or flowers which have been cut down, need to be viewed from above and are best positioned on a hearth, flower or coffee table: this is a particularly effective way of displaying large dense flowers such as peonies or groups of dainty smaller flowers such as daisies. And if you wish to group a series of containers together, make sure they are not all the same height so you avoid a regimented row.

CONTAINERS

A variety of different containers is essential equipment for the flower arranger. The container has a great effect on the appearance of the display, both on its scale and shape and in terms of style.

Containers, however, do not need to be expensive. If you do possess crystal vases or fine ceramics, these may well lend a special elegance to a display. But equally useful is a range of more humble everyday containers, from jugs and pots to baskets and bowls. Inexpensive glass "tanks" or cylinders in different sizes are indispensable and suit many applications — except displays consisting of certain flowers, such as stock, which discolour the water.

In the summer, the choice of container can reinforce the link with the outdoors. Baskets always have an informal country look and there is a wide range available in the shops, from fine painted wicker to the more overtly rustic, woven from coarse grasses, vines and even dried roots and herbs. Baskets can be waterproofed by lining them with plastic before adding oasis, or used to conceal water-filled jam jars.

Also summery are a variety of garden containers, such as terracotta pots and bowls and even watering cans. If you are arranging a flowing, trailing display in oasis, however, the appearance of the container is of little

Left: The warmth of the brick floor and wooden furniture is set off by an arrangement of brilliant reds and pinks in a copper trough. Stock, astilbe and dahlias are supplemented by copper beech, moss and driftwood for a dramatic, yet informal effect.

29

importance since it will be hidden. Plastic florist's trays, saucers or plates all make suitable reservoirs.

As far as the height of the container is concerned, tall flowers with individual florets growing well down the stem, such as gladioli, do need tall upright containers. But remember that most flowers can be cut down to suit, which may even prolong their life. And since many summer flowers are fairly bushy and full, a container with a flared neck is more practical than one with a narrow neck. A flared neck also promotes a freer look.

TYPES OF ARRANGEMENT

Almost any shape or style of arrangement can be created using the summer palette. Flowers tend to be longer-stemmed in the summer than at other times of the year, with more foliage, which extends the scope considerably as far as height and width of the arrangement are concerned. Trailing and climbing species allow displays with flowing lines to be created very easily. In fact, in summer, the "natural" look could not be simpler.

Before you begin, it is a good idea to observe how flowers really grow. No garden consists of flowers arranged in neat triangular shapes or Hogarthian curves. Instead, species are clustered together, there are gently curving sprays of buds and tiny new growth tapering away at the edges. To recreate this sense of the garden group species together, a strategy which also has the effect of helping the flowers "read" better from a distance. Place the larger flowers in the centre, the smaller towards the edges, and use trails or tendrils to break up the lines: blunt edges are unknown in nature.

When creating a vase arrangement, measure the flowers against the container to estimate how much to cut from the stems. It is important to lay each flower against the container at the angle in which it will be used, to arrive at the correct length. It is often best to begin arranging at the rim of the container, so that the stems of the outer flowers provide support for the larger central flowers which will stand upright.

It is sometimes assumed that by promoting a "natural" approach to flower arrangement, I am somehow

Right: Tall arrangements suit locations where their full beauty can be appreciated, such as this window recess. Here delphiniums, longiflorum lilies, achillea, roses and silvery lichen create a study in white.

Left: Floating in a glass bowl of water, rose heads and petals create an evocative if short-lived display. Water arrangements are most effective positioned where they will catch rays of sunlight.

rejecting the art of traditional floristry. It is true that many of these rules of proportion and construction, together with the emphasis on creating formal, symmetrical shapes, can result in contrived and artificial-looking displays. But many of the florist's skills and techniques merely extend the creative range: chicken wire, oasis and water vials are just tools of the trade. You can use these tools and apply traditional rules (many of which are based on common sense) to produce natural and spontaneous displays.

Two conventions are worth considering. One is to allow one and a half times the height of flowers to container. This gives stability to the display and provides a good depth of water so that flowers get the nourishment they need. Another useful rule-of-thumb is to combine flowers in odd numbers — threes, fives and sevens — which avoids the static look that compositions of even numbers can produce.

But rules are meant to be broken and summer is an excellent time for exercising a little ingenuity. Broken flower heads, which might otherwise be discarded, can be floated on water in a low bowl, making a stunning table centrepiece evocative of Eastern water gardens. Unusual combinations of pebbles, moss and garden vegetables can add a depth of texture to summer flowers. Single-colour displays can be given extra emphasis coordinated with fruit: for a modern, graphic look, set a bowl of marigolds beside a pyramid of lemons.

Potted Daisies

Daisies are simple, almost stylized flowers, perfectly at home in locations such as this period house which has been treated to a modern facelift. The unusual containers — a watering can and two cake tins — make a witty setting for the potted plants, their silvery colour a complement to the chrome accessories.

FLOWERS AND FOLIAGE

Potted daisies (esterides)
Bun moss

MATERIALS

Watering can
Two shaped cake tins
Plastic lining
Brick

METHOD

1   Water the pots thoroughly by submerging until bubbles stop rising to the surface.
2   Line the cake tins in plastic sheeting to prevent rusting.
3   Place a brick or similar inside the watering can to act as a support for the pot plant.
4   Place the potted plants in the containers, padding out with plastic if necessary.
5   Lay bun moss on top to disguise the pots.

CARE

The arrangement will last about two weeks. Every five days, take the containers to the sink, rewater and drain.

Textural Display

This study in textures was inspired by a grey flagstone floor and was designed to look sculptural, as if it had been carved. The pearlized onion skin, dull sheen of the flower-like succulents and grey lichen (reindeer moss) are set off by the pure white agapanthus and the glossy leaf. Reindeer moss is available dried from florists and dried flower suppliers. Once submerged in water, it expands to a springy consistency.

FLOWERS AND FOLIAGE

White agapanthus
Succulent cactus, cut
   from plant
Reindeer moss
White-skinned onions
Bun moss
Glossy garden leaf

MATERIALS

White dinner plate
Oasis
Wire or short sticks
Hairpins

METHOD

1 Soak the dried lichen (reindeer moss).
2 Place the soaked oasis on a dinner plate. Place a few glossy leaves around the edge of oasis.
3 Start at the base. Position two succulent "branches", one higher than the other.
4 Attach lichen around the succulents with hairpins.
5 Insert wires or sticks into onions and place small clumps around the succulents, piling up to the centre.
6 Tuck in more lichen to keep the onions stable.
7 Place the agapanthus at the top, at different heights.
8 Cover the edge of the plate with bun moss.

CARE

Although the agapanthus will need to be changed after about one week, the rest of the arrangement will last a couple of months, provided the oasis is kept moist.

Sweet Peas

It is always effective to respond to the context of a display. Here, an interesting pattern of light and shade on a white cotton blind is echoed in the square containers and fragility of the sweet peas, arranged to form a graded colour band across the sill. Crossed stems make a graphic silhouette against the window.

FLOWERS AND FOLIAGE

Sweet peas, ranging from pale to dark pink

MATERIALS

Three square glass containers

METHOD

1   Fill the containers with water.
2   Arrange the display so that the palest flowers are in one container, the next darkest in another and the very darkest in the last.
3   Start at the outside of the container, resting flowers on the rim.
4   Allow stems to cross so that they provide a means of support for the middle flowers, which should stand upright.

CARE

Florist's sweet peas will last longer than those cut from the garden — about one week. Change the water daily and avoid using flower food if using glass container, as food will discolour water.

Riotous Mixture

The rich surroundings of an old English manor house and topiary garden are brought to life by a vibrant combination of late summer flowers, arranged as if just gathered from an abundant border. Clashing colours give a sense of vitality and depth.

FLOWERS AND FOLIAGE

As great a variety of seasonal flowers as possible, such as:

Sunflowers
Rudbeckias
Echinops
Scabious
Asters
Cornflowers
Phlox
Marguerites
Antirrhinums
Montbretia
Golden rod
Sprengeri fern, cut
    from plant

MATERIALS

Sturdy low oval basket
    with handle
Plastic lining
Three blocks of oasis

METHOD

1 Line the basket with plastic to prevent seepage.
2 Stand the blocks of soaked oasis in the basket, so they protrude several inches above the top.
3 Establish the width and height of the display by placing tall flowers at these three points.
4 Fill towards the centre, placing larger flowers in the middle to form a focal point.
5 Group heads for impact. Insert flowers to fall down over the edge of the container, breaking the line and creating a more informal effect.

CARE

Water the oasis daily. The display will last about one week to ten days. Discard flowers which die earlier.

All In White

In a strictly monochrome setting, the temptation is to create a simple, stark arrangement of white flowers, such as lilies. Here, a softer, summer atmosphere has been generated by mixing different white flowers. Arranging the display in an aluminium watering can takes the edge off the formality. ˙

FLOWERS AND FOLIAGE

Oriental lilies
Delphiniums
Antirrhinums
Veronica
Lazianthus
Achillea
Copper beech leaves

MATERIALS

Watering can

METHOD

1   Fill the watering can with water.
2   Start at the outer edge. Rest the daintier flowers on the rim of the container, crossing stems.
3   Build up towards the centre, placing the larger flowers in the middle, the taller at the top.

CARE

If positioned in a cool location and with flower food added to the water, some of the display will last up to two weeks, particularly the lilies. Change the water as frequently as possible.

Hot Colours

Colours such as magenta and bright yellow, which are not normally combined, have been used to create a vivid, stylized display which draws attention to a picture. The simple glass containers, invaluable in many applications, do not compete in terms of style.

FLOWERS AND FOLIAGE

Three doronicums
Deep pink achillea

MATERIALS

Two square glass containers

METHOD

1. Divide achillea into two equal bunches.
2. Mass each bunch in your hand so that the heads form a flat dome.
3. Measure against the containers and trim the stems blunt so that the heads will rest on the rim.
4. Fill the containers with water and place a bunch of achillea in each to form a solid hummock of colour.
5. Insert the three doronicum in one display – they will be supported by the achillea.

CARE

The achillea will last 10 days, if the water is changed. You can replace the doronicum with other tall flowers.

Summer Hearth

Commercially grown roses, with their straight stems, can look rather formal, more reminiscent of the florist's than the garden. But if colours are mixed and the flowers are arranged without any real design or line, the look can be much more summery and abandoned. The trailing ivy suggests climbing garden roses.

FLOWERS AND FOLIAGE

Roses: "Champagne", "Bridal Pink", "Pittica", "Pink Sensation", "Gerda"
Lilac
Ivy
Laurel leaves

MATERIALS

Plastic lining
Blocks of oasis

METHOD

1   Line the base of the grate with plastic sheet.
2   Stand blocks of soaked oasis in the grate.
3   Starting at the top, insert tall roses in a haphazard way. Fill downwards, projecting roses out in an arc, inserting stems through the grate.
4   Insert lilac to spill down at the corner.
5   Position laurel and ivy at the base, allowing ivy to trail on to the floor.

CARE

This arrangement will last about five days if watered daily. Mist with a plant water spray.

Blue Elegance

The aquamarine walls in this formal room suggested an elegant arrangement of blues; this precise shade is difficult to match exactly so a spectrum of tones was chosen, with the container accentuating the colouring. Delphiniums need to be displayed tall and positioned where their full beauty can be appreciated. This display is high enough to balance the height of the table and fill the tall window.

FLOWERS AND FOLIAGE

Delphiniums
White lazianthus
Clematis trails
Roses: "Blue Moon"
Bun moss

MATERIALS

Wide oval bowl and matching plate
Oasis

METHOD

1 Fill the bowl with soaked oasis, to stand 4 inches (10cm) above the rim.
2 Build height with delphiniums, grouping in cluster. Bring delphiniums down in a gradual arc to break the line of the bowl.
3 Position open rose heads in centre as a focal point. Insert lazianthus on the same level.
4 Cover exposed areas of oasis with bun moss.
5 Position clematis so that heads rest on container and trail over.

CARE

If watered daily, this display will last about five days.

Low Arrangement

Peonies are luscious flowers, with balls of velvety petals that are especially delightful in low arrangements. Cutting heads low is one of the easiest ways of creating impact. The flowers should be massed in a dome, but not too evenly, otherwise the arrangement will look as if it has been tipped out of a mould. Recess some of the heads, by pushing the stems in further, to provide depth.

FLOWERS AND FOLIAGE

Peonies: "Sarah Bernhardt"
White hydrangea
Peony foliage
Variegated ivy

MATERIALS

Twisted vine basket
Plastic lining
Oasis

METHOD

1 Line basket with plastic sheeting.
2 Build up soaked oasis to a height of 3 inches (8 cm) over the top of the basket.
3 Cut hydrangea and peony stems to about 8 inches (20 cm).
4 Begin at the centre, inserting peonies and foliage.
5 Position peonies around the edge at 12 o'clock, 20 past and 20 to. Fill in between.
6 Fill in with hydrangea.
7 Add ivy strands around the edge and in the centre.

CARE

If watered daily, this display will last about five days.

Eastern Richness

Colour rather than content is the key to creating an arrangement that suits the style of a particular room. The burnt reds and intense blues in this display are the colours of late summer, a perfect match for the typically glowing shades in Oriental rugs. The sandy pebbles tone with the dull gold of the carpet; the water-filled bowl suggests heat and Eastern water gardens.

FLOWERS AND FOLIAGE

Delphiniums
Red lilies
Echinops
Veronica
Variegated Pittus

MATERIALS

Blue bowl
Pebbles
Oasis

METHOD

1   Layer the base of the bowl with pebbles. Place the soaked oasis on top and surround with pebbles.
2   Build height with delphiniums, keeping within confines of container.
3   Insert veronica in clusters.
4   Zigzag downward in stages: echinops, lilies, foliage.
5   Fill the bowl with water.

CARE

Top up with water daily. The display will last up to one week.

Summer Weddings

Summer is the bridal season, and a busy time for florists. Even in our unreliable climate, there is still the possibility of a bright warm day for the wedding.

If the summer months are the traditional time for weddings, pastels are still the most popular wedding colours – light, summery shades which are an appropriate choice for sunny weather. Unlike spring, the breadth of the summer colour range means that coordinating flowers with dress is easily achieved.

Summer flowers can also be adapted to suit different styles of wedding. There are many which are suitable for wiring into headdresses and bouquets, but also a good number of softer flowers which work particularly well in tied bunches.

Left: White gladioli florets, yellow roses, white hydrangea and variegated ivy combine to make a refreshing summer bouquet and headdress.

Right: White is a popular choice of colour for wedding flowers; the triangle or front-facing arrangement is a classic, formal style. Here the usual severity of the shape has been softened by wayward trails of ivy. Flowers include scabious, campanula, stock, hydrangea, alchemilla mollis, and stefanoitis, which has the added bonus of a lovely perfume.

CHOOSING WEDDING FLOWERS

Life span is a particular problem in summer. Wedding celebrations which go on all day, especially if the weather is warm, inevitably mean that by the evening the flowers are beginning to suffer.

Certain flowers, no matter how appropriate or personally meaningful, will simply not last well in bouquets or headdresses, especially if they are wired. A bouquet can take an hour and a half to make and must often be delivered to the bride at least two hours before the wedding so that there is enough time for the hairdresser and photographer to do their work. This means that by the time the wedding party is ready for the ceremony, the flowers will have already been out of water for nearly four hours. One solution is to opt for a tied bunch which can be refreshed by placing it in water for a while. Another alternative, especially for hot, dry climates, is to arrange the bouquet in a posy holder. This device, shaped like an ice-cream cone, holds a ball of soaked oasis into which the flowers are inserted. A certain amount of care is needed to prevent the flowers from getting knocked and falling out. The handle of the holder is bulky and ugly, so trails need to be arranged to cover the view of the handle. Posy holders are not a substitute for the craft of wiring but they do extend the life of a bouquet where temperatures are extreme.

Left: The rich colours of late summer are displayed in this wired circlet, for bride or bridesmaid, composed of anemones, Virginia creeper, rosehips and ivy.

SUITABLE SUMMER FLOWERS AND FOLIAGE

Agapanthus   Use individual florets or bells in wired work for headdresses or bouquets.

Alchemilla   Fresh colour and hazy look makes a good alternative to gypsophila.

Alstroemeria   Despite the delicate appearance of these lily-like flowers, they have an excellent life span when wired.

Chrysanthemums   Choose the single varieties for a summery, dainty look.

Clematis   The flower is not reliable but trails are good for bouquets.

Delphiniums   Individual florets are good for wired work.

Eucalyptus   Silvery foliage makes an excellent foil for blue or white colour scheme.

Geraniums   White or pink flowers work well in mixtures; leaves of the lemon variety add a sense of texture and scent.

Gerberas   Stark, bold flower for modern or sophisticated style.

Gladioli   Individual florets resemble orchids and are excellent in wired headdresses and bouquets.

Gypsophila   A classic wedding flower, with a hazy, dainty look.

Honeysuckle   Beautifully perfumed trailing flower for bouquets.

Hosta   Deep green or variegated large leaves, excellent for bouquets and bunches.

Hydrangeas   Lace-cap variety has a floating, hazy appearance. Good blues and pinks. Use small sections or bracts.

Ivy   Strong, well-defined leaf, excellent for bouquets. Trails add a sense of movement. Symbolizes fidelity and the 'lasting bond of marriage'.

Jasmine   Softens the line of bouquets; lovely scent.

Lavender   Old-fashioned, scented flower for bouquets.

Lilies   Excellent wedding flower despite the unfortunately persistent association with funerals.

Marguerites (daisies)   A hardy flower, simple and fresh.

Nigella   Delicate flower suitable for tied bunches. Common name is the romantic love-in-a-mist.

Pansies   Very delicate but can be wired.

Peonies   Luscious velvety petals but only suitable for tied bunches.

Pinks   Excellent for wired work. Very long life span, scented.

Roses   Invaluable wedding flowers; good colour range, scent and life.

Scabious   Lovely blue flower; use with care in wired bouquets.

Sedum   Use sections of green or pink florets.

Senecio   Silver leaf makes a useful foil for white.

Skimmia   Good hardy foliage.

Spiraea   Hazy, dainty flowers and foliage.

Stocks   Can be used wired or in tied bunches; scented.

Sweet peas   Delicate flowers in pastel shades. Commercial varieties last well.

Sweet Williams   All-purpose flower with good lifespan.

Trachellium   Flat-topped flower. Available in a dark blue which gives depth to blue and white bouquets. Use in tied bunches or wire bracts individually.

THE BRIDE'S FLOWERS

Wedding flowers must display a sense of unity. As well as bouquets for the bride and her attendants, there are corsages and buttonholes for family members, church decorations and reception displays to consider, and wide differences of colour, design or type of flower could easily result in visual chaos. This is not to suggest that there must be rigid coordination, just that subtle variations on a theme are better than an outright divergence of styles. In fact, flowers are an ideal way of creating a wedding theme and can express different moods very powerfully, from country informality to city sophistication.

In practical terms, it is best to develop ideas for the bride's flowers first. The bride is the focus of attention throughout the day and it is vital that her flowers suit her personality and appearance. This means taking into account her colouring, height and size – as well as her wishes. But above all, it means planning the flowers to suit the style of the wedding dress. Bouquets and headdresses should always be discussed after the dress is designed or chosen.

Wedding dresses and outfits vary enormously, although, in the summer, lighter fabrics such as lace, silk and tulle may well predominate. In general, full, flowing styles, with ballgown skirts, trains and veils, need to be complemented by fairly large bouquets that will sway and move with the dress. Trails of ivy, honeysuckle or jasmine are good ways of adding the required sense of movement.

Wired bouquets can be created in a wide range of shapes, including the ever-popular shower bouquet, but they must never be rigid or stiff. There is nothing worse than the sight of a bride holding a tightly wired and immobile bouquet that looks more like a shield than a bunch of flowers. For traditional wedding dresses, with a hint of Victoriana, an old-fashioned posy with rings of flowers might be appropriate. The handle can be tied with trails of lace. A summer country wedding in a simple setting could be accentuated by adopting a green and white scheme, making use of the wide range of interesting summer foliage and the variety of white

Right: This traditional posy or dome-shaped bouquet has been wired but in such a way as to give an informal, natural look. White roses, pinks, blue scabious and lucky white heather make a soft, pastel combination.

flowers available at this time of the year. Alternatively, the right note of informality can be struck by assembling a tied bunch, using flowers such as single chrysanthemums, pinks and nigella (love-in-a-mist) to suggest a country meadow. Softer summer flowers work particularly well in tied bunches; these are best carried at an angle through the crook of the arm, rather than held directly in front. And in summer it is particularly charming and natural to wear flowers in the hair, in wired circlets or small clusters worn to one side.

However tempting it may be to opt for safe and expected wedding flowers, such as roses and gypsophila, choosing less frequently seen species can help to make the day something special. Peonies are excellent summer wedding flowers and one of my favourites. Luscious, with a deep ball of velvety petals, they are just as romantic as roses. And they come in a range of good pinks which suits many summer wedding schemes. The hazy appearance of alchemilla makes this flower a good alternative to gypsophila, and its vivid yellow colour makes a sharp fresh accent which enlivens and combines well with many other shades.

FLOWERS FOR THE ATTENDANTS

Once the bride's flowers have been selected, those for the attendants and family members can be considered. Adult bridesmaids often carry a version of the bridal bouquet, but smaller and less elaborate. The colour of the bridesmaids' dresses can be accentuated by adding flowers in that shade to the bouquets.

Child attendants are always appealing. I love to see children carrying flowers which are really designed to suit them rather than to reinforce the importance of the occasion. No matter how well drilled, the behaviour of small children is always a little unpredictable, and giving them flowers which are fun to carry can inspire more cooperation. Tiny baskets filled with daisies, garlands carried between several children and hoops bound round with flowers and ivy are all intriguing and easy for small hands to manage. Wired circlets and ivy pinned round the waist look delightful on little girls.

Right: Heavy circlets of open pink roses, sweet peas and scabious look angelic on child bridesmaids. Full, wide headdresses which can be worn low on the forehead are actually more comfortable and easier to manage than narrow, dainty bands of flowers that need the added attention of hair pins.

For other family members, it is a nice idea to coordinate their flowers with the bridal bouquet. Women can wear corsages – once again back in fashion – using some of the bridal flowers; for men, rose buttonholes make a change from the ubiquitous carnation.

FLOWERS FOR THE CEREMONY

Even on a blazing hot day, the interior of a church, synagogue or registry office may well be fairly dark. Wedding decorations should accordingly be light and bright enough to be visible from a distance and positioned at strategic points for impact. Blues are difficult to handle well, and in dark interiors they tend to disappear. But the preponderance of more suitable whites, pinks and golden yellows in the summer palette mean that this is hardly a restriction.

Economy is another consideration. Few budgets are unlimited and it is likely that the bride's flowers, together with those of her attendants, will account for much of the expense. But effective displays can be created without necessarily relying on commercial flowers. Common or garden flowers can stand in for more expensive varieties – coordinating the colour or style of the flowers with the bridal bouquet will ensure that the sense of unity is not lost. The abundance of garden foliage in the summer means that, if necessary, much material can be obtained free. A green and white scheme, for example, could include pew end displays of grasses and ivy, tied with white ribbon. Strewing peony or rose petals along the aisle is also highly effective and costs very little, if you choose flowers that are past their best.

Floral archways are especially evocative, either decorating a main entrance or framing the view of the bridal pair at the altar. Although these look elaborate, many can be created fairly simply and make an imaginative alternative to the traditional pedestal-style arrangement. Displays for pew ends can be treated in different ways – the flowers can be attached to the side of the pew, trailing down, or extend up from a container on the floor. It is important to remember to ask permission before you attach anything to church fittings.

Left: A striking pedestal display is composed of hydrangea, alchemilla, wheat and ivy; many of the same ingredients have been used to decorate the altar rail, creating the impression of a fence overgrown by ferns and creepers.

FLOWERS FOR THE RECEPTION

One of the reasons that summer is a popular time for weddings is that there is at least a chance the day will be blessed with fine weather. In reliable climates, outdoor wedding parties can be planned confidently; elsewhere, it is often safer to hedge one's bets and provide a marquee or awning for shelter. But whatever the weather, flowers can help to bring a sense of the outdoors to the occasion.

Flowers for the reception should be dramatic, visible, but never in the way. In a crowd of guests, floor-level arrangements will only be obstructive and overlooked. The key positions for displays are at the entrance, to welcome visitors, on buffet, drinks or dining tables and surrounding or decorating the cake – all locations where the photographer is likely to be busy. Architectural details may inspire original and eye-catching displays, such as a garland winding down a stairway, baskets hanging from a marquee roof or trailing foliage wound round marquee poles. Again, simple ideas can be both striking and cost-effective. Strands of ivy can wind along buffet tables; low bowls with a few floating flower heads make refreshing centrepieces; and trays of drinks or canapés can also be decorated with petals or flower heads.

Right: A traditional shaped display of white and cream shades. Arum and cream lillies, stock, roses, antirrhinum, gladioli, dille, solomon's seal and foliage gently blend with the muted surroundings to create a sophisticated, elegant display.

Floral Arch

A rambling floral arch decorates a simple country church, framing the view of bride and groom. Petals are sprinkled down the aisle to form a pathway and the entire effect is warm and summery rather than grand and ostentatious.

FLOWERS AND FOLIAGE

Peonies
Pink gypsophila
Ivy
Sphagnum moss
Bun moss

MATERIALS

Weathered strips of wood (part of a latticed fence)
Terracotta pots
Quick-drying cement
String
Tacks

METHOD

1   Cement upright posts into terracotta pots with quick-drying cement.
2   Build the rest of the framework by joining uneven lengths with string or tacks. Bind in the moss with the string at joins.
3   Wind ivy around framework.
4   Wedge clusters of gypsophila and peonies in between the moss.
5   Sprinkle peony petals along aisle.

CARE

The display will last for an afternoon.

Golden Glow

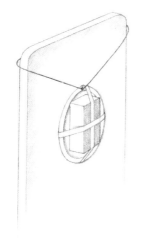

Small village churches can be quite stark and cool. This golden late summer decoration adds warmth and vitality; the contents are largely inexpensive. There are various ways of decorating a pew end; this arrangement trails from top down. Always take care when attaching displays to church fixtures.

FLOWERS AND FOLIAGE	MATERIALS
Yellow lilies	Oasis
Alchemilla	Plastic trough
Corn	Screwdriver or pointed tool
Variegated privet	Wire
Sphagnum moss	Water-resistant tape
Bun moss	Hairpins

METHOD

1 With the screwdriver, make a hole in one end of a round plastic trough. Thread wire through and hang trough on pew end.
2 Attach the oasis to the trough with water-resistant tape.
3 Insert privet and alchemilla at the top so that they ramble over the top of the pew end, but not so far that they would become battered.
4 Insert lilies in the centre, leaving oasis exposed.
5 Cover oasis with sphagnum moss and bun moss, pinning securely.
6 Pin on two sheaves of corn.
7 Insert lower flowers – trails of privet and alchemilla – facing downwards.
8 Insert two clumps of corn, one about 4 inches (10 cm) shorter than the other.

CARE

If watered daily, this display will last about a week.

Nooks and Crannies

Many churches have nooks or alcoves which can be ideal places for simple arrangements. Here a high niche is decorated with peony heads, with ivy trails to lead the eye to the display. Any substantial flower would create the right look of simplicity. This type of arrangement would also suit an entrance and is very economical.

FLOWERS AND FOLIAGE

Peony heads (or open roses)
Ivy

MATERIALS

Oasis
Plastic lining or shallow container

METHOD

1 Place soaked oasis on plastic lining or in shallow dish.
2 Insert ivy trail to one side and at the top to give height.
3 Cut three peonies to the same size and position each one facing in a different direction.

CARE

This display will last about five days if watered daily.

Bridal Bouquet

This spontaneous-looking tied bouquet would go well with a full flowing dress, especially for a country wedding. The stems are spiralled so they flare out. The scale of the bouquet makes it most appropriate for a bride but a smaller version could be created for bridesmaids or child attendants.

FLOWERS AND FOLIAGE

Peonies
Pink gypsophila
Scabious
Peony foliage

MATERIALS

Twine
Ribbon

METHOD

1 Start with the central flowers, the peonies. Attach twine to one stem, about 7 inches (18 cm) below the head to allow for a wide spread of flowers.
2 Lay the next flower at a slight angle, wrap the twine over the stems and turn the bouquet in the hand. Keep adding peonies and gypsophila. Do not over bind.
3 Add a layer of scabious until the bouquet is 5 inches (12 cm) in diameter.
4 Add another layer of gypsophila, angling the stems more the wider the bouquet becomes. Aim to achieve a dome shape.
5 Add foliage at the outer edge.
6 Trim the stems blunt, removing foliage from the binding point down. Add ribbon.

CARE

The bouquet will last well all day and can be refreshed by a drink of water.

Trailing Green

Built up from floor level, this style of pew-end decoration avoids the problem of having to attach the display. The selection of green foliage looks fresh and vital and would enhance a green and white wedding scheme. It can also be easily achieved on a limited budget.

FLOWERS AND FOLIAGE

Alchemilla
Ivy
Moss
Fern
Grasses
Beech leaves

MATERIALS

Oasis
Plastic container
Double-sided tape

METHOD

1   Place soaked oasis in container on the floor.
2   Start by inserting a clump of fern leaves at the top.
3   Arrange clumps of green grass, coming down in steps, ending with a group of beech leaves at the base.
4   Insert a tuft of yellow alchemilla at the base.
5   Cover the container with moss.
6   Trail ivy on to the floor.
7   Attach a piece of ivy on to the pew end with double-sided tape as if it were growing up the side.

CARE

If required this arrangement could last for about a week provided oasis is kept moist by watering daily. Ivy attached with tape will deteriorate earlier.

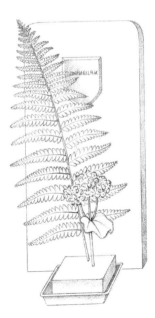

Special Occasions

The fourth of July, traditionally marked by fireworks rather than flowers, and Father's Day, are almost the only official summer celebrations. But summer is by no means short of events. In Britain, Ascot heralds the beginning of "the season", which includes the other grand society and sporting occasions of Henley and Wimbledon, as well as innumerable dances, balls and garden parties. For most of us, on a less exalted level, summer is the season of village fêtes, barbecues and picnics — a holiday time when the emphasis is on enjoying the outdoors. Flowers are a natural accompaniment to any summer occasion.

Left: To create this abundant cascade of flowers, a large stone urn has been filled with oasis built up high over the rim in a dome. Flowers are massed in a cheerful mixture of colours and include alchemilla, peonies, stock, alstroemeria, hydrangea, gypsophila, sweet william, aster and aconitum.

Right: For a garden party or outdoor event, a statue has been garlanded in flowers and fruit to lend a special magic to the occasion. Roses, godetia, limonium and grapes have been inserted into oasis bound in chickenwire. The garland is held in place by its own weight.

PARTY FLOWERS

Many summer celebrations take place outside. But even if the weather forces you indoors, a sense of the garden is important to achieve in your arrangements. It may seem superfluous to create a flower display for an outdoor party, where, after all, there are flowers growing around you, but outdoor arrangements help to promote a sense of occasion and make the event something special.

Flower displays for the garden should never be too formal. Humble containers, such as terracotta pots, simple jugs and even watering cans, strike the right note. The flowers can be chosen to reflect the colours already existing in the garden, or massed in bright country mixtures that show up well on a sunny day. This is also a good setting for combinations of flowers, fruit and vegetables – all the better if guests are encouraged to help themselves.

If the party has a theme, flowers can be chosen to provide additional emphasis. Red, white and blue displays would accent the national high spirits of a fourth of July picnic; flowers in team colours would celebrate a sporting win. Flowers can also suggest mood and atmosphere – strands of ivy and delicate white flowers would suit a romantic midsummer evening party. Pots of bright geraniums massed on a balcony or terrace can bring Mediterranean cheerfulness to lunch outdoors. A little drama never goes amiss: let your imagination suggest summer images which will bring a touch of theatricality to your displays. The displays themselves should also be exaggerated, larger than usual and prominently positioned. Group species for impact.

TABLE SETTINGS

Summer provides the ideal opportunity to combine flowers and food. Summer fruit such as raspberries and strawberries can be coordinated with deep red roses. The soft velvety skins of peaches and nectarines can be offset by alstroemeria. Cottage gardens, with their traditional combination of neat rows of vegetables and country flowers, can provide the

Left: To decorate a lunch table in the garden, a basket has been piled with a vivid mixture of fruit and flowers: stock, roses, sweet peas, artichokes, loganberries, grapes and peas. Outdoor table decorations should never be too formal or grand.

inspiration for more unusual displays of runner beans, cabbage leaves and border flowers (see page 99). Look at the massed displays of fruit and vegetables in street markets or greengrocers for ideas.

All table settings should be low so as not to obstruct views or inhibit conversation. It is also a good idea if flowers are not too heavily scented as this may interfere with the appreciation of food and wine. Never include poisonous or inedible berries in a display – guests may be tempted to sample them.

Choose naturally trailing species such as clematis or honeysuckle to wind along the table. Low bowls or platters can be used to display a few beautiful flower heads in rich warm colours, such as butter-yellow roses and apricot lilies.

GIFTS

Father's Day is one occasion which invites us to challenge the notion that flowers make suitable gifts only for women. In fact, many men now appreciate flowers – not only for Father's Day, but also as birthday and thank-you presents. There are plenty of varieties in strong, "masculine" colours and bold graphic shapes which will dispel any hint of feminity.

Although flowers make good presents in situations where a more personal gift would be inappropriate, they should not be impersonal themselves. It takes very little time and effort to make a selection which will complement the style of a person's house, the way they dress, or reflect their favourite colour. Spiralled or tied bunches are welcome gifts at parties where the host or hostess will often have little time to arrange the flowers. For the same reason, tied bunches are a good choice for hospital visits. But avoid perfumed flowers: in a confined space heavy scent can be overwhelming.

Flowers also combine naturally with other presents, such as perfume, champagne or chocolates. For a new baby, you could fill a basket with daisies and tuck a soft toy inside. Children also appreciate gifts of flowers – a scaled-down version of a Victorian posy would make a special accompaniment to a birthday present.

Right: This simple but highly effective table setting can be created in minutes. Hydrangea heads and different foliages are laid directly on the table, wound between each place and among the candelabra.

Father's Day Posy

Instead of the ubiquitous tie or pair of socks, a simple tied bunch of flowers can be a refreshing alternative for Father's Day, either as a gift in its own right or teamed with another present. Easy for a child to make, the warm strong colours, bold textures and shapes of this posy have a definitely masculine look. It is a nice idea to plan the flowers around a favourite colour scheme.

FLOWERS AND FOLIAGE

Deep red roses: "Carambol"
Yellow spray roses
Yellow celosia
Achillea
Foliage from flowers

MATERIALS

Twine
Ribbon

METHOD

1 Start with the central flower, attaching string fairly high up the stem.
2 Build up the posy, laying each flower across at an angle and binding in with the twine. Add the flowers randomly, for an informal look.
3 Knot the twine, disguise with a bright ribbon and trim the stems blunt.
4 Alternatively, mass heads together tightly in one hand and secure posy with twine.

CARE

Remove the ribbon and place the posy in water. Change the water frequently. The roses will finish first; the posy should last five to seven days.

Fruit and Flowers

A summery display, designed for a sideboard or table centre for a special evening, this arrangement emphasizes the rich tones of the wood by concentrating on warm yellows, pinks and russets. Fruit and flowers are combined in a random fashion. There are no rules; it is just a question of what looks comfortable to the eye. You can use anything to hand which fits the colour scheme.

FLOWERS AND FOLIAGE

Yellow roses
Yellow celosia
Apricot lilies
Berries
Onions
Nectarines
Pears

MATERIALS

Brass plates

METHOD

1 Place the largest plate in the centre and overlap the smaller plates across the width of the table.
2 Start at the centre plate – the highest point – and combine lily heads and fruit.
3 Gradually work down towards the edges, using smaller rose heads on the lowest plates, clustering fruit and flowers together. Combine cut with whole nectarines for textural contrast.

CARE

This is a good way of using broken heads. The flowers will only last a day or evening since they are out of water.

Doll's Tea Party

During the long summer holidays, it can be difficult to keep children amused, especially on rainy afternoons. The floral decorations for this doll's tea party are fun to do as well as educational – and need little technical skill to accomplish. A similar theme can be adapted for a birthday.

FLOWERS AND FOLIAGE

Miniature white, yellow,
    pink, red roses
Pink and cream stock
Achillea

MATERIALS

Twine
Needle and thread
Pins
Ribbon

METHOD

1   To make the doll's garland: measure around the doll's head and cut a piece of ribbon to length. Cut rosebuds so that stems are ½ inch (1 cm) long. Stitch through the seedhead or across stem to hold flower in place on ribbon. Cluster flowers together.
2   To make doll's posy: attach thread or twine 1 inch (2 cm) below head of central rosebud. Add rings of flowers in different colours, one ring at a time, binding in with string. Fasten with string or thread. Tie on to doll's hand with thread.

CARE

Out of water, the flowers will only last an afternoon, but they may dry quite well. The same effect can be achieved using dried flowers, and will last for some time if handled with care.

Summer Evening

Pale eau-de-nil walls suggested a silvery arrangement of foliage and white flowers. Fireplaces are natural focal points; for summer evening gatherings both hearth and mantelpiece can be decorated in a fresh, informal way in the light colours which show up well in fading light. Make use of any flowers in the right shades from the garden or florist.

FLOWERS AND FOLIAGE

White heather (potted)
White primula (potted)
Marguerites (potted)
Mollucella
(Bells of Ireland) potted
Variegated ivy (potted)
Silver conifer (potted)
Sphagnum moss
Silver lichen
Green lichen

MATERIALS

Pale pebbles
Plastic lining
Hairpins

METHOD

1 Water plants thoroughly and drain for one hour.
2 Line the mantelpiece with plastic sheeting.
3 Position some pots on the mantelpiece to achieve a basic line – either asymmetrically or with the highest in the centre.
4 Lay pots of ivy, heather or conifer on their sides, facing outward.
5 Fill the gaps with sphagnum moss and pin lichen to the moss.
6 Pack sphagnum moss in the front of the grate and then line with plastic. Fill with pots of marguerites.
7 On one side place white primula, and ivy so that it spills on to the tiles.
8 Cluster white pebbles and moss on the other side.

CARE

After several days, the pots will need watering. You can either dismantle the display and rebuild afterwards or water very carefully *in situ*.

Christening Garland

For a christening, it is particularly effective for a floral arrangement to reflect the nature of the occasion. Dainty displays celebrate birth better than formal or grand pedestal-type designs, and the font is a place where family members gather. This garland, made in oasis, is held in position by its weight; an ideal solution for a church, where a more permanent fixing might not be possible.

FLOWERS AND FOLIAGE

Sweet William
Pink peonies
Alchemilla
Ivy
Peony foliage

MATERIALS

Small block of oasis
Chicken wire
A few 8 inch (20 cm)
    lengths of florist's wire

METHOD

1. Cut soaked oasis into blocks, approximately 2 inches square × 5 inches long (5cm × 5cm × 12cm). (Size will depend on width of garland.)
2. Lay oasis blocks along the length of a piece of chicken wire.
3. Wrap the chicken wire to enclose the oasis. Close ends and thread wire along "seam" to enclose.
4. Lay the tube of wire and oasis in position. Cut all flowers short, leaving 1½ inch (3 cm) stems.
5. Insert flowers, working up towards ledge. Place the peony heads facing different directions – on the top and at both sides. Fill in with Sweet William, pushed in to give depth.
6. Fill gaps with tufts of vivid alchemilla and ivy, aiming to create a rounded three-quarter profile.

CARE

The garland will last a week if oasis is watered.

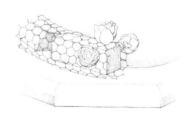

Terracotta Pots

Outdoor occasions – barbecues, garden parties, *al fresco* eating – call for displays that reflect their surroundings. Terracotta pots immediately conjure up a garden setting; vegetables and fruit suggest summer abundance. Guests can help themselves to the fruit.

FLOWERS AND FOLIAGE

4 geranium heads
Foliage from hedgerow,
    including dock leaves with
    seed heads attached
5 squash
Cherries
Loganberries or raspberries

MATERIALS

1 large terracotta pot
2 small terracotta pots
Plastic lining
Oasis
Wire
Thin garden canes

METHOD

1   Line the large pot with plastic and fill with soaked oasis, so it stands 8 inches (20 cm) above rim.
2   Work from the top, inserting foliage and clusters of dock standing about twice the height of the pot.
3   Insert geranium heads.
4   Insert a small pot into oasis by securing with a cane driven through the drainage hole.
5   Push canes into sides of squash and position around the base of the foliage and small pot.
6   Position second pot, facing opposite direction, as before.
7   Add more geranium heads, trails of foliage and place squash at base of display.
8   Pile the pots with fruit.

CARE

Water the oasis regularly. The display will last well over two weeks.

Shades of Purple

A grey stone table and a largely purple-hued garden planting suggested this impromptu table setting, designed to look overgrown. Shades of purple, from deep mauve grapes through to light lilac stock provide a graduated colour display.

FLOWERS AND FOLIAGE

Clematis
Purple stock
Limonium
Broom
Moss
Grapes
Peas

MATERIALS

Large platter
Oasis
Cocktail sticks

METHOD

1   Place soaked oasis on the large platter. Place two stock at centre top to create height.
2   Pile on grapes, wedging in place with cocktail sticks.
3   Tuck stems of limonium underneath and pile moss to cover edge of plate.
4   Extend sides with long trails. Lay grapes on table, working inwards.
5   Gently ply twists of broom into vine-like shape. Insert in oasis so that broom swirls on to table.
6   Pile clusters of moss, grapes and peas around plate.

CARE

This arrangement is difficult to dismantle and reassemble. It will last about a day without watering; about a week if watered.

Garden Party

In the height of the summer, light bleaches out colours, which makes subtle combinations less effective. This festive mixture of pink, red and yellow breaks all the traditional rules but provides a cheerful focal point for a garden party.

FLOWERS AND FOLIAGE

Nigella
Rudbeckia
Sweet peas
Echinops
Marguerites
Montbretia
Lavatera
Golden rod
Ivy

MATERIALS

Glazed earthenware jug, about 14 inches (35cm) tall.

METHOD

1 Fill the jug with water.
2 Measure flowers against the jug, at the angle at which they will be used in the display. The tallest flowers should be about twice the height of the container; the shortest just over the height of the jug.
3 Start by laying shorter flowers at the edge of the container, resting on the rim to support. Position trails of ivy and montbretia.
4 Gradually fill, clustering species together, and placing large flowers, such as rudbeckia, in the centre. Work all the way round, so that the display does not have a 'back' and a 'front'.

CARE

Rewater if possible. The display will last about six days.

Cornucopia

The rich blue-greens of this tapestry inspired a late summer combination of fruit, vegetables and flowers which tones rather than contrasts with the setting. A lavish focal point for a grand occasion, the textural nature of the displays have an old-fashioned quality.

FLOWERS AND FOLIAGE

Molucella (Bells of Ireland)
Echinops
Jacob's ladder
Ivy
Moss
Cabbages
Apples

Carrots
Beans
Onions
Pears
Aubergines
Tomatoes
Grapes

MATERIALS

Large copper cooking pot
Plastic lining
Oasis
Canes
Chicken wire
Hairpins

METHOD

For the central arrangement:

1 Line pot with plastic and pack soaked oasis to 12 inches (30cm) above rim. Cover the oasis with chicken wire to prevent crumbling.
2 Insert Jacob's ladder so it stands twice the height of the container. Group echinops below to the right; molucella to the left.
3 Pull open cabbage leaves to make flower-like. Insert sharpened canes in bases and cluster cabbages together, pushed deep into oasis.
4 Cluster aubergines and fruits on canes under molucella.
5 Break the edge with ivy trails. Pin moss at the base of the cabbages. Pin cluster of beans to overflow. Lay onions and pears at the base of the arrangement.

To make the pedestal arrangements:

1 Cover the bases of the candelabra with plastic and position 10-inch (25-cm) high pieces of oasis on top. Attach water-resistant tape to hold oasis and arrangement in place.
2 Insert one cabbage on each base to anchor the displays.
3 Pile up a selection of fruit and vegetables, securing with canes.
4 Wind ivy around the stems of the candelabra. Add clusters of beans and carrots to spill over the bases of the displays, breaking the line.

CARE

Water oasis where flowers have been used to extend life. Fruit and vegetables will slowly deteriorate; expected life approximately one week.

Basic Techniques

All cut flowers will last longer if they are properly trimmed and conditioned before arrangement; some species have special needs in this respect. In addition, there are various simple techniques, widely used by florists, which can extend the creative scope. One word of caution: wiring flowers for bouquets and headdresses is a specialist skill and requires training.

CUTTING AND CONDITIONING

Most flowers will need to be trimmed once you have arrived home. The area of the stem presented to the water should be fresh — stem ends which have been out of water for any length of time tend to dry up and absorb water less efficiently.

It is a good idea to trim at least ½-1 inch (1-2 cm) from the stems, more if the arrangement requires. Cut the stems at an oblique angle so that the largest surface area possible is available to take up the water.

Once the stems have been trimmed, put the flowers into a deep bucket of water for two hours so a reservoir can be taken up into the heads. This is especially important if the flowers will be used long-stemmed. The same advice applies equally to flowers cut from the garden or pot plants.

Above left: The formality of this triangular display is perfectly in keeping with the elegant setting. Lily heads and stock draw the eye to the centre; scabious and echinops thistles are placed towards the edges.

Right: Nothing could be easier or more suggestive of summer than this simple massed display of opening peonies.

SPECIAL CARE

Woody stems

The stems of certain flowers such as chrysanthemums and stock are fibrous and woody. To aid uptake of water, hammer the stems so they split and splinter.

Roses

Most roses come wrapped in cellophane and the heads may have wilted or dropped slightly by the time you get them home. Remove the cellophane and take off the thorns from the stems so that the flowers are more comfortable to work with. Trim the stems (they do not need to be hammered) and dip them into 2 inches (5 cm) of boiling water for 20 seconds to clear any airblocks. Then wrap the flowers in tissue paper or newspaper and place in deep water for two hours. Some of the foliage can be left on the stems to aid water absorption.

Gerbera

If stems are soft and limp, they will stiffen in water, but in a bent shape. Support upright if you want straight stems.

Allium

Change the water at least once a day to avoid strong onion smell.

Stock

Stock stems decay very quickly, making the water foul, with a strong rotting smell. Stock water should be changed at least once a day. You can add chloride (from a chemist) to the water to prolong flower life.

WATER

Cool water will prolong the life of cut flowers. In some circumstances, however, you may wish to place the flowers in warm water to open buds and bring on the display ahead of time.

The water should be as deep as the container allows. The crucial relationshp is between the length of the stem and depth of the water: the longer the stem, the deeper the water should be. Long-stemmed flowers in shallow

containers will last a fraction of their normal lifespan.

Water is an alien medium for flowers; stems drown and decompose, depositing particles which change the chemical nature of the water. To slow down the process of decay, take off the foliage below the water line and change the water in containers as frequently as possible, retrimming the stems by ½ inch (1 cm) at each water change. You can also add a flower food to the water which will make the flowers last longer, but as this yellows the water it is best not used in see-through containers. With flower food, you can change the water every three to four days; without, allow only one or two days between changes. And the warmer the weather, the quicker the water will need changing.

One of the problems of needing to change the water frequently is that you run the risk of disturbing a carefully composed and balanced arrangement. If the flowers are all in good condition, you can stand the vase or container under the tap and leave the water running until it has come up over the side. But if some of the flowers are beginning to brown, changing the water provides an opportunity to discard dead and drying heads, retrim the stems of those which survive and rearrange, perhaps in a different container. In mixed arrangements, some species will last longer than others and this is a good way of gaining maximum value and enjoyment. Similarly, flowers in bud can be arranged in a tall, elegant container; once opened, they can be cut down and arranged in a lower vase to display the heads more prominently.

Always clean containers thoroughly between use. Use bleach or a washing-up liquid and scour to remove the tidemark of algae and scum. Dirty containers only speed up the process of decay.

TEMPERATURE

It is important not to overheat flowers, especially when they are out of water. If possible, visit the florist last when you are out shopping – don't leave flowers baking on the back seat of a car while you run other errands.

Positioning is also important, especially on hot days.

Naturally warm places – sunny window sills, for example – will cause flowers to spoil quickly. Very draughty locations such as hearths and doorways can also cause problems.

If you need to take flowers on a journey, pack them in a box so they do not get crushed and add a synthetic ice pack to keep them cool and fresh. The flowers should not touch the ice pack.

USING OASIS

Oasis or florist's foam consists of a green porous material, which is available in pyramid, square and cylindrical shapes as well as the standard blocks 12 × 6 × 4 in (30 × 15 × 10 cm). Although some people maintain that oasis promotes an artificial, contrived look, it can be used to create natural-looking arrangements and is extremely useful for deep or awkwardly shaped containers. Oasis may also be the only means of creating certain shapes, such as those where flowers spill down over the edge of the container.

In some ways, oasis is a more "natural" medium for flowers than water. Oasis supports the stem in the same manner as earth or a branch. It holds a certain amount of water and presents it to the plant in the same way as earth: the flower draws as much water as it needs. Despite these advantages, flowers generally do not last as long in oasis as they do in water.

The size and shape of the oasis will depend on the arrangement, container, and the quantity and size of stems. For a display where you want the flowers to flow down over the edge of the container, the block or blocks of oasis must stand far enough above the top of the container that stems can be inserted at an upward angle. Oasis is easy to cut; odd shapes can be built up by covering blocks with chicken wire. Chicken wire wrapped around oasis will also prevent it from crumbling excessively; this is especially advisable for large arrangements where many stems are being inserted.

After the oasis has been cut to size, it should be thoroughly soaked. Float the block on top of a sink or bucket of water. The oasis will become saturated in a

Right: This strong, structured arrangement in warm summer shades consists of ripening wheat, alchemilla, alstroemeria, and lilies. Small bound sheaves of wheat are attached to the front of the basket.

matter of minutes. Do not push the oasis down to submerge it as this will cause air blocks and dry areas will remain inside.

Before you begin an arrangement, think about which direction you want the flowers to fall. Mentally divide the oasis in sections and insert the flowers in the relevant portion. Avoid crossing stems. A haphazard approach will create problems: the display will lack stability and the oasis will be more likely to break up.

Insert each stem by holding it low down and feeding it into the oasis. Do not try to insert the flower by pushing down from the head — the stem may buckle or even break. You need to insert at least 1½ or 2 inches (4-5 cm) of stem into the oasis so that the flower has a good chance of absorbing water. To insert thick stems you may have to make a hole first with a pointed tool such as a knitting needle.

The oasis should sit in a container filled with water. Top up the level daily, pouring water over the oasis as well as into the container. If the oasis is allowed to dry out, it is difficult to restore the necessary capillary action. Flower heads can be sprayed with a plant water spray. Oasis cannot be reused, but it is very cheap and widely available.

CHICKEN WIRE

Chicken wire is standard florist's equipment and has many varied uses. If a large arrangement needs to be transported, chicken wire wrapped around the oasis will prevent it from crumbling. Chicken wire also makes a good alternative to oasis for creating large displays. The wire should be crumpled and tangled so that the flowers remain stable.

For vase arrangements, chicken wire also allows you to use a few flowers, or flowers with fine stems, in a wide-necked container. If the container is opaque, a ball of chicken wire pushed down inside will hold the flowers in place. For a glass container, you can lay a mesh of chicken wire over the neck and arrange the flowers within the grid. The wire can be disguised with moss. (Alternatively, you can construct the grid with plastic tape.)

Right: A wild, rambling look for a pew end decoration: green beech, pink gypsophila, peonies, campanula, aster and variegated ivy 'grow' up from the floor.

WATER VIALS

Water vials, test tubes or "thimbles" are small glass containers of the type which are often seen enclosing the stems of orchids. They are available in four sizes to suit different stems. The special advantage of vials is that they allow cut flowers to be combined with potted displays. The vial is inserted in the earth to hold water for the cut flowers. The vial must be in an upright position and topped up daily with water. For a large arrangement, a small jam jar makes a good alternative.

WIRING

Wiring flowers consists of removing the stems and attaching lightweight wire to the flower head. The technique is mostly used for making wedding bouquets and headdresses, and for dried flower arrangements. Time-consuming, intricate, and demanding quite different skills from those used in flower arranging, wiring is best left to the professionals, especially for such important occasions as weddings.

Many people believe that wiring inevitably results in a stiff, unnatural-looking bouquet, but such rigid constructions are merely poor examples of the technique. It is perfectly possible to wire flowers so that they retain a sense of movement and fluidity. The great advantage of wiring is that it is possible to create trailing or curving shapes. And because the stems are removed, bouquets are considerably lighter and more comfortable to carry and headdresses are easier to wear for long periods. Wiring also helps avoid the flowers from becoming battered and gives extra support when they begin to wilt.

The wire must be strong enough to support the flower, but not rigid. There are over twenty gauges of wire, from fine silver for wiring tiny agapanthus florets to heavier steel for attaching large carnation heads. In a bouquet, individual wires are drawn together and taped to make a comfortable handle.

The florist will be able to advise as to which flowers are suitable for wired bouquets or headdresses. The loss of stem shortens the life of flowers and certain species such as scabious will not survive once the stems are removed.

Left: A collection of bronze figures are whimsically decorated with 'Casablanca' lily trumpets and jasmine trails.

Index

Numbers in italics refer to photographs

Acknowledgements

With special thanks to Liz Wilhide, Di Lewis, Kirsty Craven, Hilary Guy, Paul Morgan and the wonderful team at Pavilion Books, who have made working on this book such fun.

To all who have allowed me to ransack their homes for 'the sake of art', and to everyone slaving away at 56 James Street; Lucinda, Tracey, Andrea, Mark, Sam, Claire, Janine and Jayne, without whom this book would have been impossible.

To my parents, Maurice and Brenda, and my sister Jill for their never-ending support.

Finally, to Linda Smith for the 'palette' illustrations, and to Gill Elsbury for the line illustrations.

Jane Packer

The Publishers gratefully acknowledge the following for providing locations for photography:
Yve Holroyd and Lawrence Edwards, Brighton, Sussex
Mr and Mrs Elliot, Chilton Foliat, Berkshire
Mr and Mrs MacLeod-Matthews, Chenies Manor, Little Chalfont, Hertfordshire
Mr and Mrs Michael Wickham, Coleshill, Warwickshire
The Reverend Benton, St. Swithun upon Kingsgate, Winchester, Hampshire